GETTYSBURG

FOR KIDS AND GROWN-UPS, TOO!

Gregory Christianson

- Contributions by Gerald Christianson
- Oil paintings by Dale Gallon

Savas Beatie
California

© 2024 by Gregory Christianson

First edition, first printing

ISBN-13 (paperback): 978-1-61121-724-7
ISBN-13 (ebook): 978-1-61121-725-4

Library of Congress Control Number: 2024937236

SB

Savas Beatie LLC
989 Governor Drive, Suite 102
El Dorado Hills, CA 95762
Phone: 916-941-6896
(web) www.savasbeatie.com
(E-mail) sales@savasbeatie.com

Our titles are available at special discounts for bulk purchases. For more details, contact us at sales@savasbeatie.com.

To Liam, Jaden, and Jesse—my three extraordinary blessings.
Love, eternally and unconditionally.

In loving memory of my mother.

TABLE OF CONTENTS

8 · PREFACE

INTRODUCTION

12 · THE ROAD TO GETTYSBURG
▷ *MAY-JULY, 1863*

CHAPTER 1

20 · THE DEVIL TO PAY
▷ *THE FIRST DAY · JULY 1, 1863*

34 · HOLD THIS GROUND AT ALL COSTS
▷ *THE SECOND DAY • JULY 2, 1863*

78 · IT'S ALL MY FAULT
▷ *THE THIRD DAY • JULY 3, 1863*

CHAPTER 4

98 · WE WILL NEVER BE THE SAME
▷ *THE FOURTH DAY • JULY 4, 1863, and BEYOND*

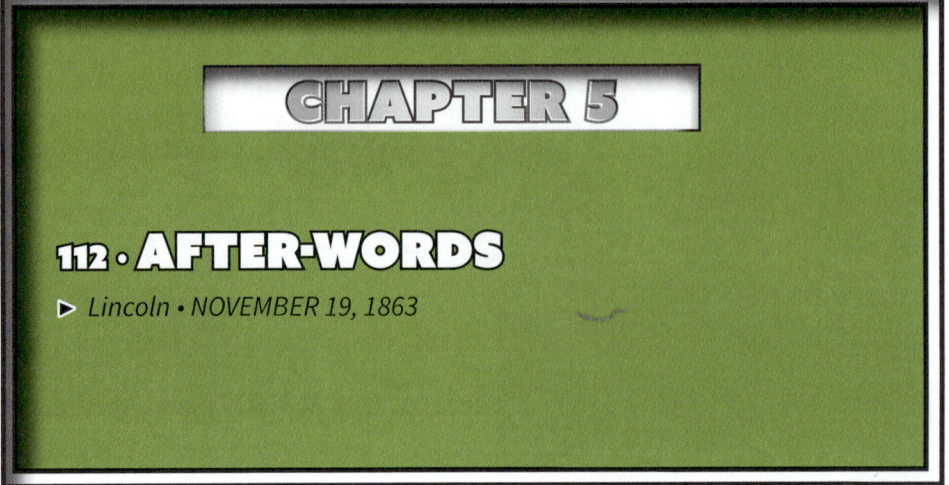

CHAPTER 5

112 · AFTER-WORDS
▷ *Lincoln • NOVEMBER 19, 1863*

122 · GLOSSARY

132 · SUGGESTED READING FOR YOUNG ADULTS

135 · SUGGESTED READING FOR ADULTS

138 · ACKNOWLEDGMENTS

139 · LAYOUT AND GRAPHIC DESIGN

140 · AUTHOR AND CONTRIBUTORS

▷ PREFACE

*Hi, I'm **JESSE**. We've got a great story for you! One of the most important in American history. And we illustrate it with original photos and paintings.*

ONE DAY LIAM AND HIS SISTER JADEN are amazed to learn that their grandfather, Gerald (left), met Albert Woolson (below), the oldest surviving Civil War soldier, whose statue now stands on the Gettysburg battlefield.

Surprised that they can touch the Civil War in only three generations, the two—now joined by their older brother Jesse—set out with their photographer-dad to explore the battle and share the story of **GETTYSBURG FOR KIDS AND GROWN-UPS, TOO!**

(L-R): **Gerald** ("Grandpa"), **Liam** ("Son"), and **Gregory Christianson** ("Pops") with the **Albert Woolson monument** on Hancock Avenue.

Albert Henry Woolson (1847? - 1956) shows a descendant, three-year-old Frances Anne Kobus, how he played a drum during the Civil War in this photo from 1953.

*From **GRANDPA** to **POPS** to me and my brothers, **LIAM** and **JESSE**—that's only **THREE GENERATIONS** to touch the **CIVIL WAR!***

GETTYSBURG FOR KIDS AND GROWN-UPS, TOO! completes the series of Kid's Books that began with **GETTYSBURG KIDS WHO DID THE IMPOSSIBLE!** and continued with **GETTYSBURG: FAST FACTS FOR KIDS AND FAMILIES!** This volume tells the story of Gettysburg itself.

Our guides—Jesse, Liam, and Jaden—invite you on a journey of discovery. Gettysburg is an amazing story! It is a true tale of heroic people struggling for the future of America.

So Kids, Parents, and Grandparents, come along! This book has something from everyone—an exciting story and lots of interesting highlights, ull wrapped in photos and paintings to show the National Battlefield as never before. Reflect, honor, learn, and have fun!

INTRODUCTION

THE ROAD TO GETTYSBURG
MAY-JULY, 1863

"Serious Work Ahead"

Painting by Dale Gallon

General Robert E. Lee

Confederate General Robert E. Lee

just won a great victory at Chancellorsville, Virginia (May 1–4, 1863). He decides it is the right time to try a second invasion of the North (the first turned back after the Battle of Antietam). His army needs food and horses. Even more, a victory on Northern soil might win support from England and France, and force President Abraham Lincoln to negotiate peace.

Lee leads his troops out of Virginia and crosses the Potomac River into Maryland and Pennsylvania. The mountains of the Shenandoah Valley provide excellent cover for his movements. But Lee is without the "eyes and ears" of his cavalry. Its commander, "Jeb" Stuart, has got himself cut off from the main force. The Confederate commander travels "blind" into enemy territory.

"For the Cause"
Painting by Dale Gallon

President Lincoln makes a bold move.

He gives the Army of the Potomac a new commander: General George Gordon Meade.

Although Meade has little experience with such large forces, he is a military engineer and knows the advantage of "good ground." He acts quickly to scout a position along Big Pipe Creek near Taneytown, Maryland, between Washington, D.C. and Gettysburg.

Federal cavalry under General John Buford moves out front to search for Lee. Buford and his troopers ride northward, on the east side of the Appalachian Mountains. They begin arriving in Gettysburg on the morning of June 30.

General George Gordon Meade

*Even before the battle starts, Lee sends troops under **JUBAL EARLY** toward York. Near Gettysburg on June 26, they run into the **26TH PENNSYLVANIA MILITIA**, including 56 students from Pennsylvania (now Gettysburg) College. After a brave but brief skirmish, they either scatter or surrender. Early dismisses them with a warning: **"GO HOME TO YOUR MOTHERS!"***

Buford statue

General Lee makes his way to Chambersburg.

Sending parts of his army as far away as the Harrisburg and Columbia areas, some cross South Mountain at Cashtown, looking for supplies. They suddenly stumble into what they think are local, untrained militia. But they are Union cavalry who quickly sound the alarm: Lee has been found! The Battle of Gettysburg—the most important in American history and the bloodiest—is on.

THE FIRST DAY: WEDNESDAY, JULY 1, 1863
CHAPTER 1 THE DEVIL TO PAY

"Heavy Task Before Us"
Painting by Dale Gallon

Daybreak—July 1st, 1863.

A blazing red sunrise greets General John Buford. Perched in the cupola atop the Lutheran Seminary, he scans the horizon west and north. Soon he will learn that 75,000 Confederates—Robert E. Lee's entire Army of Northern Virginia—is converging on this little town of ten crossroads.

Confederate units under General Henry Heth, searching for shoes and other supplies, soon begin to appear on the Chambersburg Pike. Buford realizes that whoever secures the high ground on Cemetery Hill, south of Gettysburg, will control the vital crossroads to Baltimore and Washington. He decides to make a stand.

Neither Lee nor Meade planned a battle here. But as soon as Heth's infantry and Buford's cavalry engage, there is no turning back.

General Buford

Lutheran Seminary

THE BATTLE OF GETTYSBURG BEGINS.

Two miles west of town, Lieutenant Marcellus Jones of the 8th Illinois Cavalry fires at 6,000 Confederates marching down Chambersburg Pike. It is the first shot of the battle.

Buford and his 3,000 cavalrymen dismount and fight a delaying action. Rapidly firing their carbines and six cannons, the troopers slow the rebel advance until forced to fall back to McPherson Ridge and the Seminary.

Buford sends word ten miles south to General John Reynolds to hurry the 12,000 men of his I Corps to seize the high ground before the Confederates break through. Reynolds sets out immediately.

Poor **EPHRAIM WHISLER.** The sight of Confederates marching by his house on Chambersburg Pike causes him to collapse. Sadly, he never recovers.

"Time To Fight"
Painting by Dale Gallon

Reynolds statue

By 10:00 A.M., Buford is almost surrounded

when up rides General Reynolds, who asks,

"What's the matter, John?"

"There's the devil to pay," Buford replies.

For the moment, Reynolds and Buford succeed in holding McPherson Ridge. But Heth and the Confederates finally get organized, and more units are pouring in from Chambersburg. They begin to turn the tide.

Slowing them down comes at a high cost. As he begins to get the Iron Brigade into position, Reynolds is shot from his horse.

General Reynolds

Reynold's death does not stop the Iron Brigade.

They charge into McPherson Woods with ferocity and stop the advance of Archer's Brigade, Lee's leading unit. General James Archer is a native of nearby Baltimore. He commands men from Alabama and Tennessee. Even though the "men of iron" capture Archer himself, they suffer so many casualties that the brigade can no longer serve as a fighting force.

▷ The men of the **IRON BRIGADE** come from **MICHIGAN**, **WISCONSIN**, and **INDIANA**, and boast that they are the 1st Brigade of the 1st Division of the I Corps. They are also known as the **BLACK HATS** because they wear black **HARDEE HATS**. These hats feature a brass infantry bugle, a brass eagle badge on the side to hold the brim up, and an ostrich feather plume.

"Final Glory"
Painting by Dale Gallon

UNION GENERAL OLIVER O. HOWARD

arrives late-morning and positions his XI Corps in the vicinity of the College, just north of the Town Square. Here he expects to meet the next wave of Confederates. He stretches his line from Oak Hill, where the Eternal Peace Light now stands, to the Pauper's Cemetery and Barlow's Knoll.

General Howard

A tremendous assault sweeps in from the Harrisburg area to the north, led by General Robert Rodes. Outflanked and breaking at several points, Howard's men fall back, fighting as they retreat through town. Reaching the top of Oak Hill, the Confederates are amazed. They can look down on the Union line from this point to the Seminary, and proceed to roll it up.

General Gordon

General Barlow

▷ **BARLOW'S KNOLL** gets its name from **FRANCES BARLOW**. At only 29 he looks to some like a newsboy. He is badly wounded during the retreat. **CONFEDERATE GENERAL JOHN BROWN GORDON** finds him, gives him water from his canteen, and has him cared for. Faithful to his promise, Gordon allows Barlow's wife, **ARABELLA**, to tend to her husband within the enemy camp. Some years later, Barlow and Gordon (now a senator from Georgia) meet for dinner in Washington, D.C.

DESPERATE DEFENDERS FORM A LAST STAND

behind felled trees and fence rails in front of the Seminary. Soon surrounded, one of Lt. Col. George McFarlane's "boys" carries his badly wounded commander through the north door of the Seminary as the Confederates charge through the south! With the capture of the Seminary and the rout at Oak Ridge and Barlow's Knoll, the Confederates win their greatest victory on northern soil. Can they now drive the Federals off Cemetery Ridge where they have formed a new line of defense?

▷ As dusk falls on Gettysburg, the **FIRST DAY'S FIGHTING CEASES**. Making their cooking fires, reorganizing their equipment, seeking rest after the day's victory, preparing for another fight the next day—the streets become a bivouac for thousands of Confederates. **SHARPSHOOTERS** from both sides, however, are just beginning their day. They take positions best suited for any target that might present itself.

THE SECOND DAY: THURSDAY, JULY 2, 1863

CHAPTER 2
HOLD THIS GROUND AT ALL COSTS

"Hold At All Costs"
Painting by Dale Gallon

After the chaotic fighting of the first day,

both armies settle into new positions: the Confederates on Seminary Ridge and the Union Army on Cemetery Ridge. The line extends from Little Round Top in the south to Culp's Hill in the north and around to East Cemetery Hill, and looks like a fish hook. It offers a stout defense, but is still vulnerable at the ends. General Lee could do little to organize the fighting in the early hours of July 1, but now he takes full command. He and his battle-hardened Confederates are still fresh from one of the most brilliant and decisive victories of the war at Chancellorsville and are full of confidence.

*Looking from the Union center on **CEMETERY RIDGE** toward the Confederate center and the Virginia Memorial on **SEMINARY RIDGE.***

Lee initiates a battle plan

that carried him to success at Chancellorsville. He will strike and overwhelm the Federals on one flank while keeping them occupied on the other. Lee agrees with General Richard Ewell that an assault up Culp's Hill on the right flank might be too risky. Instead, Ewell is to make a demonstration, then use his discretion about launching a full-scale attack. The main thrust will be aimed at the Union left anchored on Little Round Top.

"Tomorrow We Must Attack"
Painting by Dale Gallon

General James Longstreet,

Lee's "War Horse," is ordered to make the assault on Little Round Top. What his scouts see while examining the ground is opportunity. No Federals appear to occupy this strategic position! However, when Longstreet gets under way, he discovers that his route will put him in full view of the enemy. The general decides to reverse course and try another way. While this costs him valuable time, Union General Daniel Sickles gives him an unexpected advantage.

Longstreet statue in Pitzer's Woods

Little Round Top

Sickles Commands the III Corps

on the Union left. He is not a trained military officer but a political appointee from New York. What he lacks in skill he makes up for in audacity. He believes that the poor position of General Howard's troops led to the defeat at Chancellorsville and intends to correct any such mistake on his front.

> Before **SICKLES** becomes a general, he shoots his wife's boyfriend dead. At trial, he claims **"TEMPORARY INSANITY."** A **"NOT GUILTY"** verdict is the first in American history for such a defense.

Contrary to the orders of General Meade

to remain on the defensive, Sickles moves his entire Corps over half a mile out in front of the Union line on Cemetery Ridge. Thinly stretching his 10,000 men northwest from Devil's Den and along the Emmitsburg Road, he unwittingly exposes the entire Union left. His unsuspecting soldiers move out toward a Peach Orchard and a Wheatfield, soon giving these little-known plots of ground a permanent place in American history.

General Dan Sickles

Looking west toward the **PEACH ORCHARD.** The **SHERFY BARN** across the Emmitsburg Road can be seen on the right.

General John Bell Hood (reenactor)

Brigades under John Bell Hood

explode from the woods on Warfield Ridge, headed toward the Union left flank. Hood cries out,

"Fix bayonets, my brave Texans. Forward and take those heights!"

He is soon wounded by an exploding shell, but regiments from Texas, Arkansas, and Alabama courageously press on toward Devil's Den and Little Round Top without their commander. In the meantime, Georgians head for the Wheatfield and the "Valley of Death."

▶ Talk about taking a hit! Shortly after **JOHN BELL HOOD** begins his assault on the Union left, a shell explodes overhead. Never again can he use his **LEFT ARM.** To add insult to injury, the general loses his **RIGHT LEG** at Chickamauga and must be strapped to his horse thereafter!

Generals Meade and **Hancock** consult as fighting begins.

"Expecting a Battle"
Painting by Dale Gallon

The **TROSTLE FARM** (General Sickles' headquarters) sits closely behind the **PEACH ORCHARD** which has now become the new Union front.

General William Barksdale's Assault

General William Barksdale

directly into the front of Sickles' new line "is the grandest charge ever made by mortal man," according to a Union officer who witnesses its well-ordered fury. Barksdale's Mississippians pulverize Union forces at the Peach Orchard, shatter their line on the Emmitsburg Road, and temporarily break their center on Cemetery Ridge. Barksdale is a whole mile into enemy territory before he meets his death.

*The **MISSISSIPPI MONUMENT** on West Confederate Avenue near where **BARKSDALE** launches his attack.*

Captain John Bigelow

and his 9th Massachusetts Battery slow the charging Mississippians. Firing as they retreat toward the Trostle farm, Bigelow's men stop only to cut dead and wounded horses from their caissons. The gunners depend on the powerful recoil of the cannons to help push them backwards.

Bigelow makes a last stand at the farm, giving Union commanders the critical time needed to reposition their forces along Cemetery Ridge. Originally riding into battle atop eighty-eight horses, the survivors of the 9th Massachusetts return with only eight.

▶ Quickly made into a field hospital, the **TROSTLE FARM** has a large **CANNON BALL HOLE** in its south-facing brick work. After the battle, Catharine Trostle files a claim with the United States government, citing **116 DEAD HORSES** and all kinds of property damage. In return, the government gives her nothing.

← CHECK IT OUT!

Hood's Division Attacks

HOOD'S DIVISION ATTACKS *the boulder-strewn Devil's Den, defended by the 4th New York Battery. Eventually overrun, the battery abandons three of its cannons. As the Federals lose their hold on the Den, the Confederates pour into the adjacent Wheatfield, which becomes an all-out hot-spot.*

▷ **DEVIL'S DEN** *is the result of volcanic activity in the late Triassic Period, some 200 million years ago!*

▷ Amidst pleas to stay down, **COLONEL AUGUSTUS ELLIS** (right) and **MAJOR JAMES CROMWELL** of the **124TH NEW YORK REGIMENT** mount their horses and draw their swords, leading a counterattack to defend the **4TH NEW YORK ARTILLERY** on Devil's Den. Both men are shot dead.

THE WHEATFIELD CHANGES HANDS SIX TIMES.

It becomes known as "the whirlpool of death." As many as 20,000 men fight to control this 20-acre plot of land. Over 6,000 are killed, wounded, or captured before the Federals finally fall back.

"Pride of Erin"
Painting by Dale Gallon

> "Colonel Cross, this day will bring you a star!"
> "No, General, this is my last battle."
> (—Colonel Cross to General Hancock)

▷ Having dreamt about his own death at Gettysburg, **COLONEL EDWARD CROSS** wears a **BLACK BANDANA** into battle instead of his usual red. Cross' premonition comes tragically true in the Wheatfield when a minie ball strikes him in the stomach.

▶ After Union **GENERAL JAMES BARNES** pulls brigades out of Stony Hill—some say before even firing a shot—**GENERAL DAVID BIRNEY** gives blunt orders for Barnes' men to lie down while Zook's brigade passes over them. **GENERAL ZOOK** and **COLONEL PATRICK KELLY** drive the Confederates from **STONY HILL**, while **CROSS** clears the **WHEATFIELD** back to the edge of the **ROSE WOODS**, but not before Zook and Cross are mortally wounded. **GENERAL JOHN BROOKE** is sent in relief, but by this time the Peach Orchard has completely collapsed and **WOFFORDS'** men drive Brooke from the **ROSE WOODS**. By 7:30 p.m., Confederate brigades under **ANDERSON, SEMMES,** and **KERSHAW** are completely exhausted from hours of fighting. Semmes is mortally wounded, but Wofford's men keep driving down the Wheatfield Road until counterattacked by Union **GENERAL SAMUEL CRAWFORD** and **COMPANY K** from **GETTYSBURG**.

the departed

General Samuel K. Zook

Colonel Edward E. Cross

General Paul J. Semmes

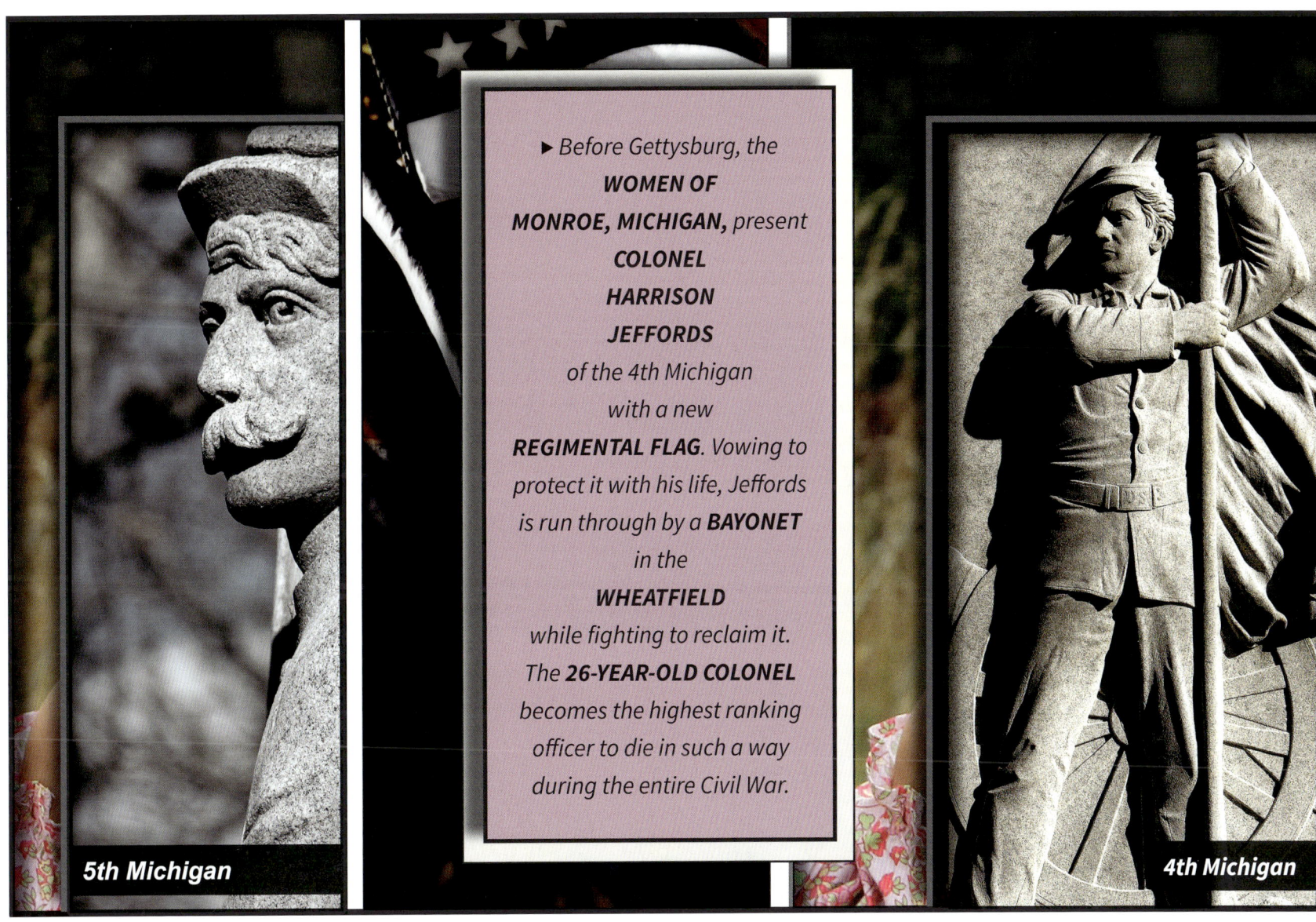

▶ Before Gettysburg, the **WOMEN OF MONROE, MICHIGAN,** present **COLONEL HARRISON JEFFORDS** of the 4th Michigan with a new **REGIMENTAL FLAG.** Vowing to protect it with his life, Jeffords is run through by a **BAYONET** in the **WHEATFIELD** while fighting to reclaim it. The **26-YEAR-OLD COLONEL** becomes the highest ranking officer to die in such a way during the entire Civil War.

5th Michigan

4th Michigan

Relentless Confederates

RELENTLESS CONFEDERATES press forward across blood-soaked fields. It's 4:30 p.m. Longstreet's infantry and sharpshooters begin to assualt Little Round Top. Victory seems within reach.

▷ **CONFEDERATE SHARPSHOOTERS** benefit from large boulders in Devil's Den (back, right) to wreak havoc on Little Round Top. **UNION GENERAL STEPHEN WEED** and **LIEUTENANT CHARLES HAZLETT** have July, 1863, on their tombstones as a result.

"Hazlett's Battery"

Painting by Dale Gallon

▷ *Exhausted and thirsty, the **15TH ALABAMA** reaches the field after marching **25 MILES** in blistering heat! **TWENTY-TWO** of them are sent for **WATER**. Unfortunately for the 15th, the regiment encounters **CHAMBERLAIN'S 20TH MAINE** before they can return. Some argue that these men might have changed the outcome at **LITTLE ROUND TOP.***

▶ Despite having his foot nearly torn off by an exploding shell, **GENERAL BARKSDALE** drives his Mississippians deep within **CEMETERY RIDGE** before a bullet finally takes his command. Shot from his horse in a counterattack led by **COLONEL GEORGE WILLARD**, the general shouts to his aide,

"I am killed! Tell my wife and children that I died fighting at my post."

Ironically, Barksdale outlives Willard by a night, as the Union colonel is soon struck dead by an artillery shell.

▷ Officially called **PLUM RUN**, this picturesque stream between **DEVIL'S DEN** and **LITTLE ROUND TOP** runs blood red through the **"VALLEY OF DEATH"** on **JULY 2**. Scores of thirsty, wounded soldiers find their way here only to bleed out in its waters. Since then, the stream is called **"BLOODY RUN."**

"What Are Your Orders?"
Painting by Dale Gallon

General Gouverneur Warren,

Meade's chief of engineers, known for his ability to anticipate danger, spots the Confederates. Warren sends a staff officer to find help.

The officer soon comes upon Colonel Strong Vincent and the 83rd Pennsylvania. Vincent sees that Little Round Top is near at hand. He decides to act without consulting his superiors, and replies, "I will take the responsibility."

With only fifteen minutes to spare, Vincent breathlessly directs over 1,300 men from Michigan, New York, Pennsylvania, and Maine into defensive positions along the top.

General Gouverneur Warren

"Little Round Top and the Valley of Death"
Painting by Dale Gallon

THE HASTILY ESTABLISHED LINE begins to break under the onslaught. Warren calls to General Stephen Weed for reinforcements. Colonel Patrick "Paddy" O'Rourke of the 140th New York says that he needs orders from his own commanders. General Warren shouts, "Never mind that, Paddy. Bring them up on the double-quick and don't stop for aligning."

The New Yorkers make a hill-saving charge down the western slope. While holding the regimental colors and spurring on his men, O'Rourke is felled by a bullet through the neck. Weed is hit by a rebel sharpshooter. And young Hazlett, as he is reaching down to offer help, is shot dead.

The Federals, however, refuse to give ground along the top, so the Confederates try to get around the side—the extreme left flank of the entire Union line. They plunge into the lower saddle between the Big and Little Round Tops.

Liam spends a quiet moment with **PADDY O'ROURKE.**

61

Already under fire

from Confederate sharpshooters at Devil's Den, Vincent seeks out Colonel Joshua Lawrence Chamberlain of the 20th Maine and declares,

"This is the left end of the Union line. You understand? You are to hold this ground at all costs!"

The costs include Vincent himself. Supported by Lieutenant Charles Hazlett's battery, Federals fire on the advancing Texans and Alabamians as they advance toward the hill.

Rebels answer and a bullet tears through Vincent, leaving him mortally wounded. His last words: "Don't give an inch!"

Colonel Joshua Chamberlain

▶ **COLONEL CHAMBERLAIN** is present at **APPOMATTOX** in 1865 to receive the surrender of the Confederate Army and is awarded a **MEDAL OF HONOR** in 1893 for his defense of **LITTLE ROUND TOP**.

"20th Maine and 15th Alabama"
Painting by Dale Gallon

Colonel Chamberlain and His 20th Maine

arrive just in the nick of time. Around 6:00 p.m., the 15th and 47th Alabama, led by Colonel William Oates, feverishly attack. Outnumbered nearly two to one, Chamberlain's 358 men absorb wave after wave. Blue and Gray alike fall in what Private Theodore Gerrish describes as "a terrible medley of cries, shouts, cheers, groans, prayers, curses, bursting shells, whizzing rifle bullets, and clanging steel."

"My dead and wounded were nearly as great in number as those still on duty," Oates reports.

Still, about 7:00 p.m., he prepares to move around Chamberlain one last time. The 20th Maine is a mere shadow of itself with only 228 men. They have exhausted every ounce of ammunition, even what they have pulled from their dead comrades. Chamberlain, the former professor, considers his choices: he dare not retreat, but he can't survive another attack. One word was enough. "Bayonet!"

As the Alabamians storm the slope, Chamberlain orders a "right-wheel forward."

"And," says Private Gerrish, "with one wild yell of anguish wrung from its tortured heart, the regiment charged."

Like a gate swinging shut, Chamberlain's left converges on the Rebel flank while his right slams down on the center. Overwhelmed, many Confederates are captured. The left anchor of the Federal line is safe at last.

"Bayonet! Forward"
Painting by Dale Gallon

1st Minnesota monument

A SECOND CONFLICT SHAKES
the Union center as the sun is dipping down. Alabamians under General Camus Wilcox surge through the breach created when Sickles advanced to the Peach Orchard.

Winfield Scott Hancock, Meade's ablest general, desperately looks for forces to fill the gap. He gallops up to William Colvill, commander of the lst Minnesota, and shouts, "Forward Colonel, and take those colors!" The hard-charging Minnesotans suffer record losses, but the stunned Confederates are stopped.

"Minnesota Forward"
Painting by Dale Gallon

General Henry Slocum (reeanctor)

More trouble brews on Culp's Hill.

Federals on the right of the fish hook must repeat Chamberlain's success on the left. Again a small unit finds itself alone, outnumbered, and on the crest of a hill. This time it's Culp's Hill above Spangler's Spring.

Union General Henry Slocum of the XII Corps has to shift troops from this area to reinforce Little Round Top because of Sickles' blunder. Yet, if it were not for Slocum—who holds back General George Greene's brigade—even fewer troops would have remained to defend the hill.

Confederate General Edward "Allegheny" Johnson sees his chance. About 7:00 p.m., nearly the same time as Wilcox's drive toward the Union center, Johnson's men march up Culp's Hill.

General Slocum, Union XII Corps commander, at the western base of Culp's Hill.

Near the top is General George Greene,

called "Pop" by his troops because at 62 he is the oldest Union general at Gettysburg. He's an engineer and he orders his men to throw up log barricades.

General Greene (reenactor)

These do the job for the roughly 1,350 defenders. Johnson's division—with over three times as many men—repeatedly attacks the hill, only to be repulsed. The result is the same as Chamberlain's more famous stand at Little Round Top. But Pop Greene remains an unsung hero. Perhaps it's because he orders barricades, not bayonets.

Greene is memorialized at the crest of **Culp's Hill.**

Building **BARRICADES** from rocks and wood isn't as popular in 1863 as you might think. Some generals believe it's "soft" and cowardly. But without **BREASTWORKS**, like the ones **POP GREENE** uses, Union defenses on Culp's Hill would be swept away by a hailstorm of bullets and a flood of men.

Pop Greene

THE BOY MAJOR OF BENNER'S HILL

▶ His men affectionately call him **"THE BOY MAJOR."** He is **JOSEPH LATIMER**, nineteen years old and the **YOUNGEST MAJOR** in the Confederate Army. He commands an **ARTILLERY BATTALION** on July 2 and told to fire upon Union forces on **EAST CEMETERY HILL**. He chooses **BENNER'S HILL** on the road to Hanover. Unfortunately, Latimer is caught in the cross fire of 40 Federal canons.

"A storm of shell greeted us the moment our first gun fired. It seemed the enemy had gotten the range of the hill even before we fired." (—Artillerist W.F. Hatton)

As young Latimer rides along the crest of the hill, encouraging his men, a **SHELL EXPLODES** nearby. He and his horse fall to the ground. The men must pull the boy major from under his dead horse. Latimer dies a month later, just two weeks shy of his **20TH BIRTHDAY**.

Major Joseph Latimer

A FINAL CRISIS LOOMS

on nearby East Cemetery Hill at the curve in the fish hook. A desperate fight ensues as Confederates strike toward the entrance of Evergreen Cemetery. For a moment they break through and fight with artillerymen around the Union guns. General Hancock rushes in reinforcements. Now in complete darkness, the two sides grapple hand to hand until the Confederates fall back and the Union line is restored.

"Night Assault"
Painting by Dale Gallon

The long day, one of the war's bloodiest

and most important, has ended. Lee's army has attacked all along the Union line—left, right, and even center—but, despite some very close shaves, the Federals hold on. That evening Meade determines to remain on the defensive. He predicts, correctly, that on the coming day Lee will strike the Union center, and this time in full force.

THE THIRD DAY: FRIDAY, JULY 3, 1863

CHAPTER 3 IT'S ALL MY FAULT

This group of figures at the base of the **VIRGINIA MEMORIAL** represent Lee's infantry, cavalry, and artillery.

General Robert E. Lee

THE MORNING OF JULY 3 DAWNS.

General Lee tries once more to turn the Federal right. This is the "barb" of the fishhook that protects Cemetery Ridge, East Cemetery Hill, and the Baltimore Pike (the main supply line to Washington, D.C.). Confederate General "Allegheny" Johnson renews the attack on Pop Greene's forces commanding Culp's Hill. Again and again Johnson's troops attempt to charge up the steep slope but each time are repelled. The furious seven-hour fight is the longest engagement during the entire battle.

"The hoarse shouts of friend and foe, the piteous cries of wounded and dying . . . war is hell!" —Major James Beall, 21st North Carolina)

General "Allegheny" Johnson

▶ *Why is Culp's Hill so important? If **GENERAL SLOCUM'S XII CORPS** doesn't hold these heights on July 2 and 3, the Union Army will likely not only lose **CEMETERY HILL**, but also its main route to **WASHINGTON, D.C.***

CEMETERY RIDGE *seen from the Culp's Hill observation tower.*

General James Longstreet

LEE IS DETERMINED TO STRIKE THE UNION CENTER.

General Longstreet protests. The army should swing around the firmly established Federals on Cemetery Ridge and get between them and Washington, D.C. where the Confederates can choose good ground and force the Federals to attack. But Lee has come to fight and Longstreet's plan sounds like a retreat. There is no turning back. He will assault the Union center around a copse of trees and an angle of stone wall.

Lee will also send his dashing cavalryman, Jeb Stuart, behind the Yankee lines to attack the rear. Unknown to Lee, however, Stuart's ride is turned back by troopers under General David Gregg and George Armstrong Custer, a very young officer who will later give his name to "Custer's Last Stand" in the West.

←Lee's Target: the Union Center on Cemetery Ridge

"Custer at Hanover"
Painting by Dale Gallon

General James Pettigrew

Longstreet forms his line of attack.

Fresh troops under Generals James Pettigrew will go on the left, Isaac Trimble in the center, and George Pickett on the right. Prospects seem good. Longstreet will send approximately 12,500 men against only about half that number of Federals. Or so it appears. Meade keeps a large number of reserves hidden nearby.

*The famous **"Copse of Trees"***

Edward Porter Alexander

Lee's Artillery Begins a Thunderous Barrage.

Colonel Edward Porter Alexander assembles an unprecedented number of cannons (approximately 150) spread over two miles. Lee hopes this will silence the Union guns and decimate the defenders. But most of the shells go too high and fall behind the Federal line. One nearly strikes the Union commander, George Meade, as he stands outside his headquarters.

Henry Jackson Hunt

THE FEDERAL GUNS REPLY FOR ONLY A SHORT TIME.

Chief of Artillery Henry Jackson Hunt and Union commanders wisely determine to halt their firing during the Confederate cannonade. This fools Southern officers into believing that their massive bombardment has done its work. It also saves ammunition for the attack that the Yankees know will come straight at them.

"Remember Old Virginia"
Painting by Dale Gallon

THE CANNONS FALL SILENT.

General Pickett orders his men forward, calling to arms the brigades of Lewis Armistead, Richard Garnett, and James Kemper:

"Up men and to your posts! Don't forget today that you are from Old Virginia!"

The Confederates have to march over an open field and up a steady slope for nearly a mile, climb fences along the way, and finally charge over a stone wall.

▶ *To the casual observer standing opposite the **COPSE OF TREES** and **THE ANGLE**, the terrain doesn't appear to be particularly difficult, but for those who march across this no-man's land, it's a different story.*

General John Gibbon

THE FRONT LINE OF PICKETT'S CHARGE IS OVER A MILE WIDE

and targets the very center of Hancock's II Corps. Union General John Gibbon's division is in the middle, with Alexander Hays' division to the north and Abner Doubleday's I Corps—those who took the brunt of the attack on the First Day—to the south.

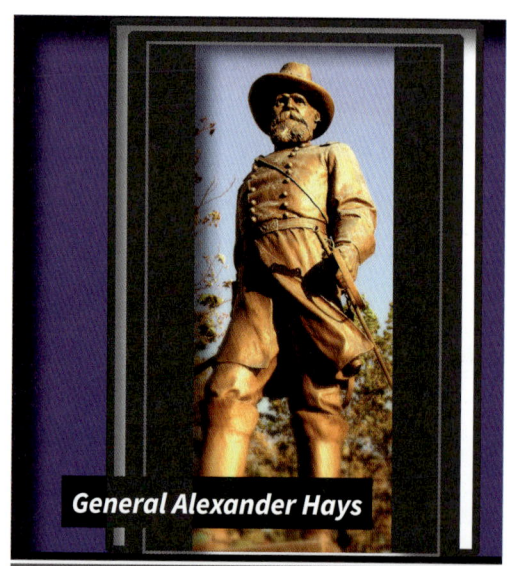

General Alexander Hays

General Abner Doubleday

General Winfield Scott Hancock

AS THE CONFEDERATES COME WITHIN RANGE, the Union artillery opens up with devastating effect. First comes cannister, shells filled with round metal balls, then grapeshot with anything from nails to glass. The effect is like a giant shotgun. The hail of shells makes it almost impossible for Trimble and Pettigrew to cross the Emmitsburg Road. On the opposite side, General George Stannard's 2nd Vermont Brigade marches out, turns right, and fires directly into Kemper's flank.

General Lewis Armistead

Still the Confederates press forward,

only to be met by withering rifle fire. From behind the stone wall Hays' men line up four deep, exchanging places as they fire and fall back to reload.

"The storm of lead and iron seemed to fill the air, as in a sleet storm, and made one gasp for breath."

(—Sargeant John Eakin, 28th Virginia)

Despite all this, roughly 200 Confederates storm the wall and break through at the Angle, led by General Armistead waiving his hat on the point of his sword.

"The Day Is Ours"
Painting by Dale Gallon

***F**OR ONE TERRIBLE MOMENT the battle hangs in the balance. Union General Hancock throws in his reinforcements. General Alexander Webb rushes to close the gap in the Union line with the Philadelphia Brigade, the 69th Pennsylvania, and Colonel Norman Hall's 7th Michigan. Wounded in the leg, Webb stays on the field and repulses the attack. Armistead, Hancock's old West Point comrade, is mortally wounded and Pickett's charge is doomed—along with the hopes of the Old South. This is the High Water Mark of the Confederacy, the furthest point that the Confederate Army will reach on the battlefield of Gettysburg and in the entire Civil War.*

General Alexander Webb

"Fire at the Angle"
Painting by Dale Gallon

THE ASSAULT LASTS LESS THAN AN HOUR.

Of the roughly 12,500 men from Virginia, North Carolina, Mississippi, Alabama, Tennessee, and Florida who set off on Pickett's Charge, over 50% become casualties. All three of Pickett's commanders—Armistead, Garnett, and Kemper—are among them.

Lee rides out to meet the survivors as they straggle back to Seminary Ridge. He calls out to Pickett to ready his division for a Union counterattack. Pickett sadly replies,

"General Lee, I have no division." To the others, Lee declares, "It's all my fault."

"Sad Day to Us"
Painting by Dale Gallon

THE FOURTH DAY: SATURDAY, JULY 4, 1863, AND BEYOND

CHAPTER 4 WE WILL NEVER BE THE SAME

Soldiers' National Monument

It's the Fourth of July. The battle is over.

Roughly 23,000 Union and 28,000 Confederates are killed, wounded, missing, or captured during three days of fighting—almost as many Americans as the entire Vietnam War. To this day, it remains the largest battle ever fought in the Western Hemisphere.

▷ Over **167,000** Americans fought at Gettysburg and somewhere between **46,000** to **51,000** became casualties. That's roughly one out of every three.

LEE AND THE CONFEDERATE ARMY ARE GONE,

retreating down the road to Virginia. They are followed by a seventeen-mile train of wagons. Lee's retreat carries 8,000 wounded. Another 6,800 are left behind because they are unfit for travel. After midnight and in a driving rain, General Custer and the 6th Michigan Cavalry charge Lee's rear guard as they are crossing over South Mountain. They capture dozens of wagons and over 1,300 prisoners, most of whom are wounded. But the Confederate army escapes.

Jeb Stuart and his troopers continue to fight off Union probes. The much-admired General Pettigrew is killed. Forced to halt and build pontoon bridges over the flooded Potomac River, the Confederates dig in and await a counterattack, but the exhausted Federals never come in force.

South Mountain in the Appalachian chain as seen from **Little Round Top.**

Jeb Stuart

Just imagine! Badly **WOUNDED** Confederates are forced to endure **HEAVY RAINS**, and bounce along on **ROUGH ROADS** over the **MOUNTAIN**. And the wagons have no suspension!

One invasion has ended. Another is about to begin.

The trickle of people arriving in Gettysburg grows daily as streams of families, anxious to determine the fate of their husbands and fathers, sons and brothers, turns into waves when railroad service is restored.

The town bears the same battle scars as the fields and ridges around it. Over 30,000 wounded soldiers of both armies occupy temporary shelters when the battle finally ends. These are not "hospitals," but private homes, churches, barns, warehouses, and every other usable building within ten miles of Gettysburg. The townsfolk—men, women, and children, black and white—must tend to the wounded and bury the fallen.

Dead horses, mules, and soldiers lie where they fell—some in shallow graves but all decomposing in the July sun. Piles of decaying flesh, evidence of the surgeon's blade, can be found next to the makeshift hospitals. Over-taxed privies assault the senses.

"Steeped in Sorrow and Death"
Painting by Dale Gallon

Help is on the way.

Merchant buildings, emptied by their owners as the Confederates advanced on Gettysburg, become depots for food and medical supplies. Fahnestock's store serves as the temporary home of the U.S. Sanitary Commission from which wagons are dispatched to supply hospitals scattered around the region. John Schick's store on the Square serves as the main depot of the United States Christian Commission.

The Sisters of Charity travel from Emmitsburg to lend their nursing skills. They are a religious order founded by St. Elizabeth Ann Seton. Their distinctive headdresses look like flying nuns. As they make their way to Gettysburg, Sister Camilla is stunned:

"O, it was beyond description! Hundreds of both armies lying dead almost on the track that the driver has to be careful not to pass over the bodies."

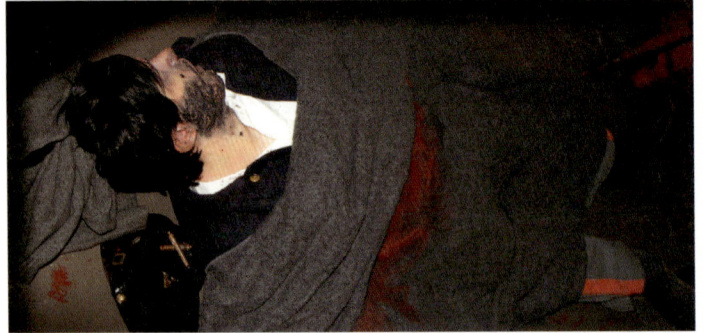

A FIELD HOSPITAL CALLED CAMP LETTERMAN

takes shape east of Gettysburg along the York Road. It is named for Dr. Jonathan Letterman, the Medical Director of the Army of the Potomac. By August he closes all the smaller, make-shift hospitals and turns Camp Letterman into the largest field hospital ever built in North America. Its patients include as many as 14,000 Union and 6,800 Confederate soldiers. Camp Letterman remains in operation until Lincoln's visit in November.

Letterman praises the 650 medical officers who were present during and after the battle and who served day and night, with little rest, until July 7.

"The labor performed by these officers was immense. Some of them fainted from exhaustion, induced by over-exertion."

Not all the wounded can be saved. Burials near the camp are a daily routine. Still worse, heavy rains expose the shallow graves all around the battlefield. Troubled by this, Gettysburg attorney David Wills petitions the federal government to establish a decent burial ground. On his own, he purchases land on Cemetery Hill. The local Evergreen Cemetery is on the east side of the new property—the former for civilians, the latter for war veterans. This becomes the Soldiers' National Cemetery. It is the first national cemetery and the first to be laid out according to a plan. The bodies of Union soldiers will be organized by state and regiment—if they can be identified.

To move the bodies,

local businesses offer bids. The government awards the contract to a farmer, F.W. Biesecker, who employs Samuel Weaver as Superintendent of Exhumation. Weaver hires a number of African-American laborers, including Basil Biggs who lives near Gettysburg and probably served as a "conductor" on the Underground Railroad.

The dead are not easily identified. They do not have "dog tags." In addition, the work has to wait until cooler weather. The tedious job begins on October 23. Progress is slow at first because, as Weaver reports,

"Many of the graves were opened and partially or carelessly closed."

Weaver's crews remove the bodies from their makeshift graves. They mark, identify, and transport the bodies to the cemetery. The work is only partially completed when Lincoln attends the dedication of the National Cemetery on November 19. It is finally finished during the following Spring, 1864, when the last soldier is given a resting place—a total of 3,512 reburials.

*Confederates have to wait until 1871 when **SAMUEL WEAVER'S SON, RUFUS,** helps return the **REMAINS OF 3,320 SOLDIERS** to the South. There are so many that **RICHMOND'S HOLLYWOOD CEMETERY** has a **GETTYSBURG HILL**!*

LINCOLN • NOVEMBER 19, 1863

CHAPTER 5

AFTER-WORDS

Train Station

David Wills

ATTORNEY DAVID WILLS PLANS A GRAND CEREMONY

for the dedication of the Soldiers' National Cemetery on November 19, 1863, and invites President Abraham Lincoln to deliver "a few appropriate remarks." Contrary to popular legend, Lincoln does not scribble his speech on the back of an envelope while riding the train to Gettysburg, but he does put some finishing touches on it later in the day.

He steps off the train in early evening. A large crowd of well-wishers, perhaps a thousand or more, is there to greet him. A group of soldiers from what is known as the "Invalid Corps" accompany him to the Wills House on the Town Square. The crowd follows him and later gathers beneath his window after he retires to his room. A band asks what he would like to hear. "Dixie," he responds to everyone's surprise. It's a sign that he hopes that enemies will soon again be one.

In the morning Lincoln takes a ride out toward the Seminary to view the place where General John Reynolds fell. Having seen the battlefield, he revises his speech once again. About 10:00 a.m. he emerges from the Wills House and waits for the parade to form. As with many parades, there are military units and civic groups, but also dignitaries, including Governor Andrew Curtin and Secretary of State, William Seward.

At 11:00 a.m. they are ready to go.

They march up Baltimore Street to Cemetery Hill—close to where Union and Confederate troops fought hand to hand as darkness fell on July 2—and enter the new National Cemetery by the west entrance.

They proceed to the platform located about halfway between today's Soldiers' National Monument and the iron fence along Evergreen Cemetery. As many as 15,000 persons are in attendance.

Prayers and music come first. Then the featured speaker of the day—the distinguished orator Edward Everett—begins. He takes two hours to deliver his speech.

"Musician"
Painting by Dale Gallon

Now Lincoln rises to give his "remarks."

The New York Times reports that Lincoln reads his speech from a sheet of paper in his hand. He speaks in a "deliberate manner, with strong emphasis," and "in a clean, loud tone of voice" that can be heard at the back of the crowd. His remarks are short, less than three minutes. He is surrounded by over a thousand graves in a cemetery that is still incomplete in a war that is not over.

Is it all worth it? This is **LINCOLN'S** challenge.

His answer recalls the Declaration of Independence.

The dead gave their lives to preserve the promise that "all men are created equal." They died to preserve a nation that is "the last best hope of earth" because in 1863 this is the world's only democracy.

His ringing words and powerful plea for dedication to "a new birth of freedom" give fresh meaning to the Declaration as the young Republic tries to find its way amidst all the suffering and death of war. These same characteristics make "the Gettysburg Address" known around the world as one of the great speeches in human history.

President Lincoln

John Burns

Secretary Seward

Governor Curtin

AFTER A LATE LUNCH AT THE WILLS HOUSE, Pennsylvania's Governor Curtin hosts a reception for the president. Lincoln stands at the front door greeting the guests. Among them is Gettysburg hero John Burns.

It is late afternoon when the Marine Band accompanies Lincoln, Burns, and other dignitaries to the Presbyterian Church where the president meets with a group of political supporters. Shortly after 6:00 p.m. he walks to the railway station for the return trip to Washington. Coffins in freight cars still await burial.

What he leaves behind will never be the same: the people, the town, America itself. The nation that was founded in Philadelphia has found out who it is in Gettysburg.

It is rather for us to be here dedicated to the great task remaining before us—that from these honored dead we take increased devotion to that cause for which they gave the last full measure of devotion—that we here highly resolve that these dead shall not have died in vain—that this nation, under God, shall have a new birth of freedom—and that government of the people, by the people, for the people, shall not perish from the earth.

Abraham Lincoln
November 19, 1863

GLOSSARY

ABOLITIONIST - A person who wants to eliminate or "abolish" slavery.

ANTEBELLUM - "Before the war." Used to decribe the United States before the Civil War.

ASSAULT - A forceful attack.

BREASTWORK - A quickly constructed defensive work, often made of logs and stones.

BARRAGE - Concentrated rifle or artillery fire.

CARTRIDGE - The paper casing that contains a bullet and gunpowder for a rifle.

CARTRIDGE BOX - A container worn on a soldier's belt for carrying rifle cartridges.

CASUALTIES - Soldiers who are wounded, killed, missing, or captured.

CONFEDERACY - Another name for the Confederate States of America. Also known as the South.

COPSE OF TREES - The grouping of trees that are the target of Pickett's Charge.

COUNTERATTACK - *an attack that responds to one by the enemy.*

Watercolor by Gettysburg artist Tom Rooney

COURIER - *A soldier who carries mail or messages.*

DEPOT - *A train station or a place to store supplies such as food and ammunition.*

DIXIE - Nickname for the South derived from the popular song "Dixie."

FEDERALS - Soldiers in the Union army.

HARDTACK - Crackers made from flour, water, and salt.

HAVERSACK - A bag that soldiers use to carry food and other items. ▶

LADLE - a long-handled spoon used for serving soup or water.

MASON-DIXON LINE - The boundary that runs between Pennsylvania to the north and Virginia, Maryland, and Delaware to the south. It often symbolizes the divide between free and slave states.

MEMORIAL - Something, such as a statue or a monument, that reminds us of persons or events.

MILITARY ENGINEER - A person trained to build defensive works and suggest the best ground for maneuvers.

MILITIA - A force of lightly-trained civilians used during emergencies.

MINIE BALL - A bullet used in muskets that is rifled and allowed to spin.

MUSKET - A long gun with a smooth bore that soldiers shoot from the shoulder. ▶

REBEL - A nickname given to Confederates.

REVEILLE - The bugle call that wakes the troops.

ROLL CALL - Checking attendance. After a battle it tells who has survived.

▲ **SKIRMISHERS** - Soldiers who are placed out front of the main force.

STANDARD - A flag or banner carried into battle.

STRATEGY - A "game plan." The highest level of planning during a war or battle.

SEMINARY - A school of higher education, such as a private school for girls or for preparing ministers.

TACTICS - Specific maneuvers during a battle to help achieve the "game plan."

TAPS - The last bugle call of the day, often played at military funerals and memorial events. ▶

TROOPER - A soldier in the cavalry.

UNDERGROUND RAILROAD - A network of secret routes and safe houses used by slaves to escapte into free states.

UNION - The states that remained loyal to the United States. Also called the North.

VOLLEY - To fire a number of weapons at the same time.

SUGGESTED READING

SUGGESTED READING FOR YOUNG ADULTS

Anderson, Tanya. *Tillie Pierce: Teen Eyewitness to the Battle of Gettysburg.* Twenty-First Century Books, 2013.

Catton, Bruce. *The Golden Book of the Civil War.* Adapted for young readers by Charles Flato. Golden Press, 1961.

Christianson, Gregory. *Gettysburg! Fast Facts for Kids and Families.* Savas Beatie, 2021.

Christianson, Gregory. *Gettysburg Kids Who Did the Impossible!* Savas Beatie, 2019.

Herdegen, Lance J. *Union Soldiers in the American Civil War.* Savas Beatie, 2018.

Hughes, Mark. *Civil War Handbook: Facts and Photos for Readers of All Ages.* Savas Beatie, 2019.

Hughes, Mark. *Confederate Soldiers in the American Civil War.* Savas Beatie, 2017.

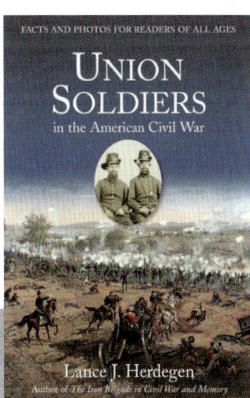
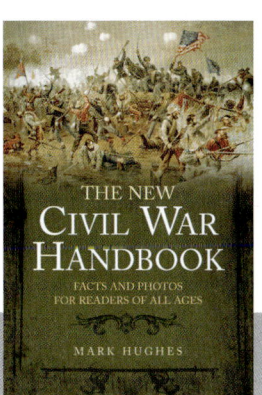
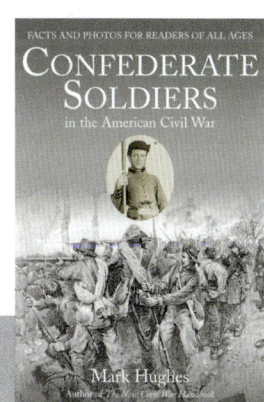

Klein, Lisa M. *Two Girls of Gettysburg.* Children's Books, 2008.

Martin, Iain C. *Gettysburg: The True Account of Two Young Heroes in the Greatest Battle of the Civil War.* Sky Pony Press, 2013.

Miller, Bobbi. *The Girls of Gettysburg.* Holiday House, 2014.

O'Connor, Jim. *What Was the Battle of Gettysburg?* Grosset & Dunlap, 2013.

Ratliff, Thomas. *You Wouldn't Want to Be a Civil War Soldier! A War You'd Rather Not Fight.* Franklin Watts, 2004.

Tarshis, Lauren. *I Survived the Battle of Gettysburg, 1863.* Scholastic, 2013.

Venner, William Thomas. *Young Heroes of Gettysburg.* White Mane Kids, 2000.

SUGGESTED READING FOR ADULTS

Adelman, Garry E., and Timothy H. Smith. *Devil's Den: A History and Guide.* Thomas Publications, 1997.

Boritt, Gabor. *Gettysburg Gospel: The Lincoln Speech that Nobody Knows.* Simon & Schuster, 2006.

Catton, Bruce. *Gettysburg: The Final Fury.* Vintage Books, 2013.

Christianson, Gerald, Barbara Franco, and Leonard Hummel, Editors. *Gettysburg: The Quest for Meaning.* Seminary Ridge Press, 2016.

Coco, Gregory A. *A Strange and Blighted Land. Gettysburg: The Aftermath of a Battle.* Savas Beatie, 2017.

Coddington, Edwin. *The Gettysburg Campaign: A Study in Command.* Simon & Shuster, 1997.

Coleman, W. Stephen. *Discovering Gettysburg.* Savas Beatie, 2017.

Frassanito, William A. *Gettysburg: A Journey in Time.* Scribner, 1975.

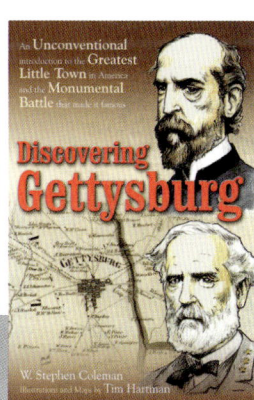

Gramm, Kent. *Gettysburg: A Meditation on War and Values.* University of Indiana Press, 1994.

Guelzo, Allen. *Gettysburg: The Last Invasion.* Vintage Books, 2014.

Hessler, James A., and Wayne Motts. *Pickett's Charge at Gettysburg: A Guide to the Most Famous Attack in American History.* Savas Beatie, 2015.

Hoch, Bradley R. *The Lincoln Trail in Pennsylvania: A History and Guide.* Penn State University Press, 2001.

Mackowski, Chris, Kristopher D. White, and Daniel T. Davis. *Fight Like the Devil: The First Day at Gettysburg.* Savas Beatie, 2015.

Mackowski, Chris, Kristopher D. White, and Daniel T. Davis. *Stay and Fight it Out: The Second Day at Gettysburg.* Savas Beatie, 2019.

McPherson, James M. *Hallowed Ground: A Walk at Gettysburg.* Zenith Press, 2015.

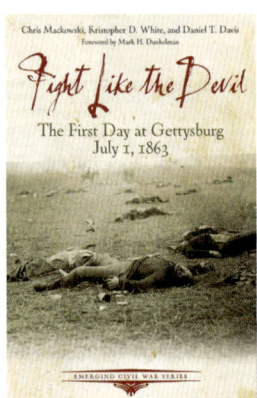
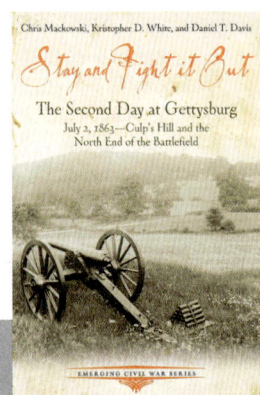
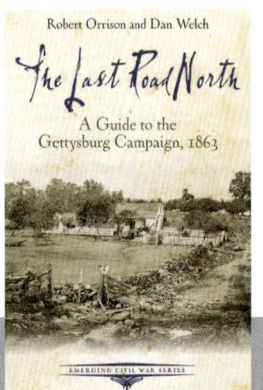

Orrison, Robert, and Dan Welch. *The Last Road North: A Guide to the Gettysburg Campaign, 1863.* Savas Beatie, 2016.

Petruzzi, J. David. *The Complete Gettysburg Guide.* Savas Beatie, 2009.

Pfanz, Harry W. *Gettysburg: The Second Day.* University of North Carolina Press, 1987.

Reardon, Carol. *Pickett's Charge in History and Memory.* University of North Carolina Press, 1997.

Shaara, Michael. *The Killer Angels.* Modern Library, 2004.

Wittenberg, Eric J., and J. David Petruzzi. *Plenty of Blame to Go Around: Jeb Stuart's Controversial Ride to Gettysburg.* Savas Beatie, 2006.

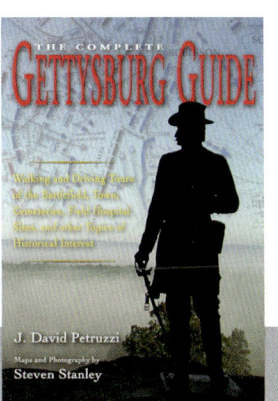
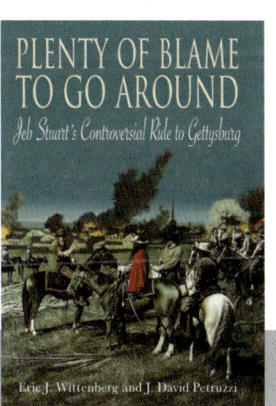
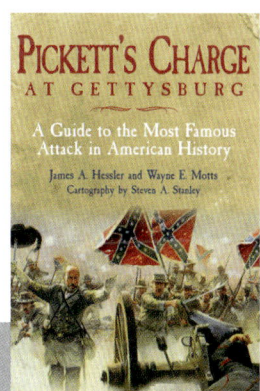

acknowledgments

Extraordinary thanks to my family • Tom Rutherford • Kerie Horan-Noll • Terry Fox • Kelly, Marissa, and Abby Sandoe • April Schilpp • Alan Natali • Tom Rooney • Matt Crowner • Susan Colestock Hill • Civil War reenactors the world over • Gettysburg National Military Park Visitors Center • Adams County Historical Society • Gettysburg Seminary Ridge Museum • StoneSentinels.com • "The Gettysburg Experience" and its editor, Diana Loski • Gettysburg Heritage Center • Bradley Hoch • Dale and Anne Gallon • Taryn Kerper • my publisher, Theodore Savas, for seeing the possibilities in this project, and Sarah Keeney for guiding it through to completion.

layout and graphic design

• Gregory Christianson

photo credits

• Gregory Christianson

with additional photos by Taryn Kerper (30-31; 89; 91, lower right; 94, upper left; 100, lower; 131, lower), and others in the public domain, courtesy of the Library of Congress (10, lower left; 14; 16; 22, upper right; 27; 28; 30; 31; 41, upper right; 44, lower left; 52; 56, upper right; 62; 71, lower right; 73, upper right; 80; 81, upper left; 82, upper left; 84; 86, upper left; 87, upper left; 92, upper left; 100, upper right; 103, upper right; 105; 107, lower right; 110; 114, lower left; 115; 118; 119; 132).

photo editing and manipulation

• Gregory Christianson

oil paintings

• Dale Gallon

The modern photographs in this book are meant to capture the imagination. They may not replicate in specific detail every place or person referred to, whether civilian or military, including their units, ranks, uniforms, or costumes.

AUTHOR & CONTRIBUTORS

GREGORY CHRISTIANSON

▶ *is an author and photographer, lives in Gettysburg, and has been walking the battlefield near his home since he was a child. Greg is the former publisher and editor of the award-winning UNSUNG HERO MAGAZINE, and the author of the well-received GETTYSBURG KIDS WHO DID THE IMPOSSIBLE! (Savas Beatie, 2019), and GETTYSBURG! FAST FACTS FOR KIDS AND FAMILIES (Savas Beatie 2023), and THE RECONCILIATION OF ALL THINGS (Xlibris, 2010). He keeps fit by tramping the battlefield in search of the perfect photograph and by coaching and playing soccer at every opportunity.*

GERALD CHRISTIANSON

▶ is Professor Emeritus of Church History at United Lutheran Seminary, Gettysburg, co-editor of *Gettysburg: The Quest for Meaning*, and contributor to *Gettysburg Kids Who Did the Impossible!* and *Gettysburg! Fast Facts for Kids and Families*.

DALE GALLON

▶ has painted over 300 historical images since 1980. His paintings appear in the Gettysburg Seminary Ridge Museum and in *Gettysburg Kids Who Did the Impossible!* and *Gettysburg! Fast Facts for Kids and Families*.

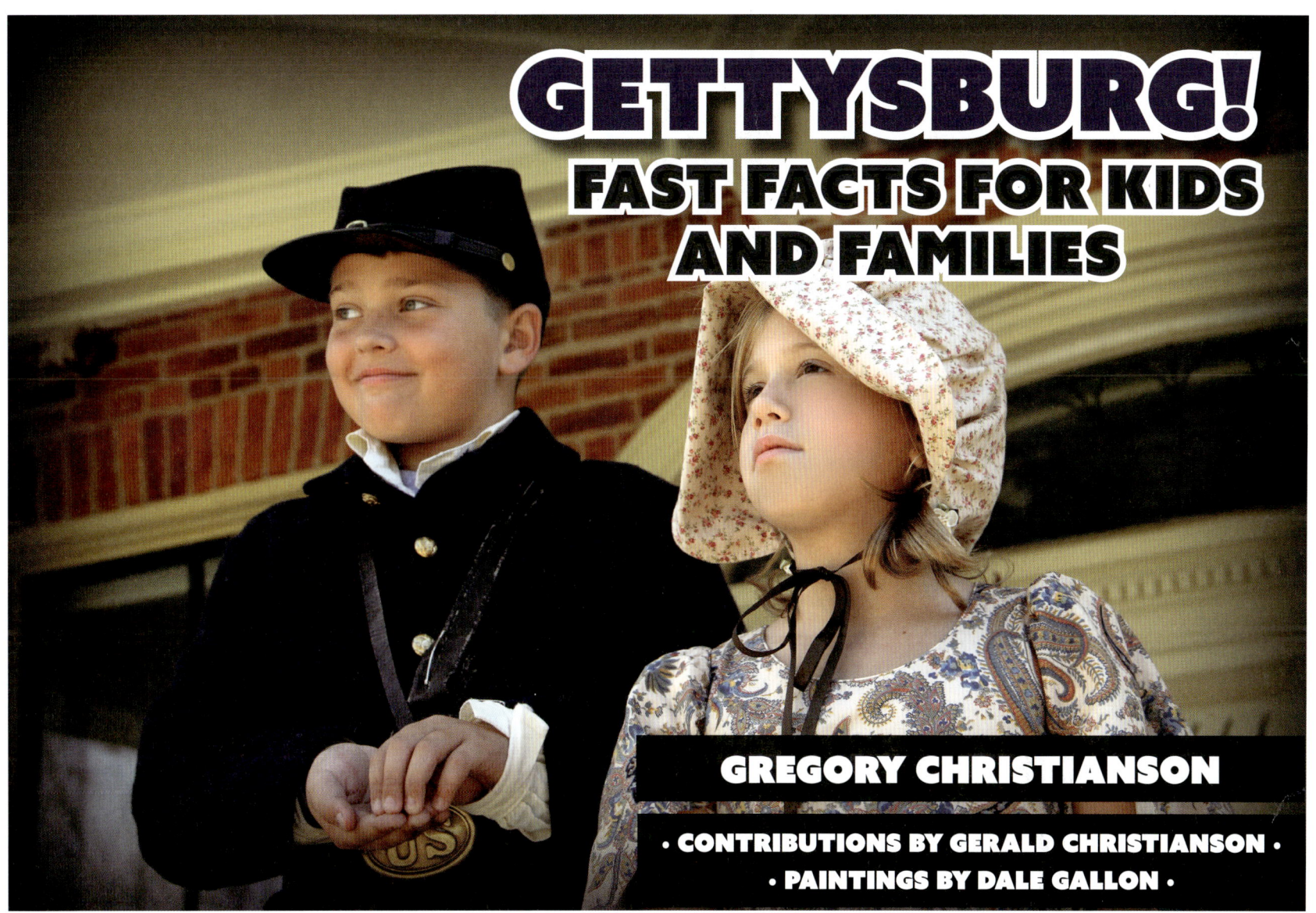

www.Facebook.com/GettysburgKidsBook